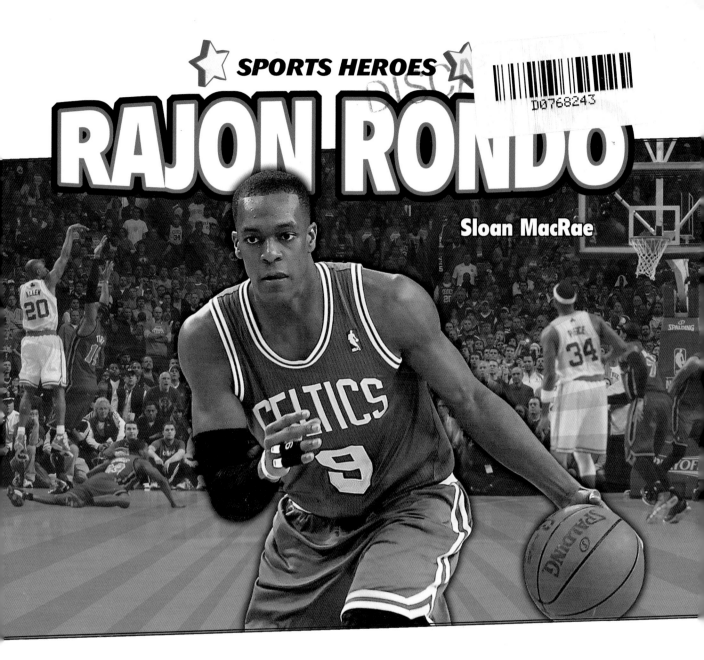

SPORTS HEROES

RAJON RONDO

Sloan MacRae

PowerKiDS press™

New York

Published in 2012 by The Rosen Publishing Group, Inc.
29 East 21st Street, New York, NY 10010

First Edition

Editor: Jennifer Way
Book Design: Julio Gil

Photo Credits: Cover, p. 5 Nick Laham/Getty Images; cover (background), pp. 7, 13, 22 Elsa/Getty Images; p. 4 Greg Nelson/Sports Illustrated/Getty Images; p. 6 Marc Serota/Getty Images; pp. 8–9 Manny Millan/Sports Illustrated/Getty Images; pp. 10, 11 Andy Lyons/Getty Images; p. 12 Gary Dineen via NBAE/Getty Images; pp. 14, 19 Jesse D. Garrabrant/NBAE via Getty Images; p. 15 (left) Brian Babineau/NBAE via Getty Images; p. 15 (right) Kevin C. Cox/Getty Images; pp. 16, 17 Nathaniel S. Butler/NBAE/Getty Images; p. 18 Kevork Djansezian/Getty Images; p. 21 Jordan Strauss/WireImage/Getty Images.

Library of Congress Cataloging-in-Publication Data

MacRae, Sloan.
  Rajon Rondo / by Sloan MacRae. — 1st ed.
      p. cm. — (Sports heroes)
  Includes index.
  ISBN 978-1-4488-6165-1 (library binding) — ISBN 978-1-4488-6288-7 (pbk.) — ISBN 978-1-4488-6289-4 (6-pack)
  1. Rondo, Rajon. 2. Basketball players—United States—Juvenile literature. I. Title.
  GV884.R6185M33 2012
  796.323092—dc23
  [B]
                                          2011026810

Manufactured in the United States of America

CPSIA Compliance Information: Batch #WW12PK: For Further Information contact Rosen Publishing, New York, New York at 1-800-237-9932

# CONTENTS

BASKETBALL SMARTS

Most people think they know what it takes to be a basketball star. You have to be tall. You have to able to **shoot** well. Rajon Rondo shows that you also have to be smart.

Rondo is the **point guard** for the Boston Celtics. A point guard is the leader of the basketball team. All good leaders have to be smart, and Rondo is one of the

Rondo's job as point guard »» is to lead his team's offense. He makes sure that the ball gets to players who have an opening to score.

smartest point guards in the National Basketball Association, or the NBA. He creates moments for his team to score by **passing** the ball to the right player at the right time. He is also great at **stealing** the ball from players on the other team.

‹‹‹ Here is Rondo (center) trying to score against the Chicago Bulls in a 2011 game.

BORN IN KENTUCKY

Rajon Rondo was born in Louisville, Kentucky, on February 22, 1986. He and his family lived in a poor part of the city. There was lots of crime in their neighborhood. Rajon has two brothers and one sister. Amber, Rajon's mother, worked hard to raise four children.

Rondo has always enjoyed sports and games. In fact, he plays some of his favorite childhood games in their Wii or iPhone versions.

Basketball was important to the children in the Rondo family's community, so Amber bought them a basketball hoop. When the weather was bad, the neighborhood kids came to their house to play board games like Battleship, Monopoly, and Connect Four. Amber knew it was important to keep her family active so that they would stay out of trouble.

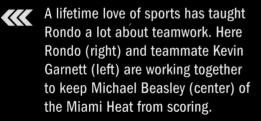

A lifetime love of sports has taught Rondo a lot about teamwork. Here Rondo (right) and teammate Kevin Garnett (left) are working together to keep Michael Beasley (center) of the Miami Heat from scoring.

55 POINTS!

As a kid Rajon enjoyed playing baseball, football, and basketball. He loved being the pitcher in baseball, the quarterback in football, and the point guard in basketball.

Rajon's 55-point game was the second highest all-time for points scored in a game at Oak Hill Academy. Here is Rondo at the McDonald's High School All-American Game in 2004. This is an annual game played by the best high school players in the United States.

Rajon was skinny as a teenager. He did not have the build to be a football player, so he decided to focus on basketball during high school. Rajon entered Eastern High School in Middletown, Kentucky, in 2000 and played there for three seasons. In 2003, he moved to Oak Hill Academy in Virginia for his senior year and became one of the best high-school basketball players in the country. In one game, he scored 55 points!

Rajon decided to go to the University of Kentucky and play for the Wildcats in 2004. This gave him the chance to work with a great **coach** named Orlando "Tubby" Smith. Rondo and Smith respected each other, but they did not always get along. Smith had a plan for how he wanted each game to go. Rondo liked

Here is Rondo shooting the ball during a 2005 game against High Point University. »»

to change things up when he felt the moment was right.

Rondo spent only two years with the Wildcats. It was enough time to set the school record for the most steals in a season. In 2006, Rondo felt that he was ready to be a **professional** basketball player in the NBA.

 During his freshman year at the University of Kentucky, Rondo set a school record of 87 steals. Here is Rondo (right) in a 2005 game against Lipscomb University.

TAKING A CHANCE

Rondo was a great college player, but not very many NBA teams were interested in him. His shooting skills were not at the level of other professional players. It was known that he did not always listen to his coach. Some teams thought these were problems.

Rondo was the first point guard chosen in the 2006 NBA Draft. The Celtics thought Rondo was a promising player who would help the team out of its slump. »»

The Boston Celtics had their eyes on Rondo during the 2006 NBA **Draft**. They watched team after team pass on the chance to take him. Finally, the Phoenix Suns selected Rondo. The Celtics made a deal with the Suns, and Rondo went to Boston. The Celtics took a chance by making a deal to get Rondo.

 Rondo needed to work on his shooting skills during his rookie year with the Celtics. Here he is successfully dunking during a 2007 game against the Milwaukee Bucks.

Rondo did not start for the Celtics until partway through his rookie season. Head coach Doc Rivers (right) wanted Rondo to prove himself on the court before he moved him to a starting spot.

The Celtics have one of the richest histories in the entire NBA, but in Rondo's first year, they were one of the worst teams in basketball. Rondo did not get the starting point guard spot, but he did impress the coach and his new team with his excellent play.

Rondo became one of the best **rookies** in the NBA. Rondo was soon known for making assists. An assist happens when

Here Rondo (center) makes a layup against the Cleveland Cavaliers during a game near the end of his rookie season.

a player passes the ball to another player who scores. Rondo got better and better during his rookie season. He recorded lots of steals and assists. Fans in Boston were excited about their team's new point guard.

Rondo played better and better as his rookie season went along. Here he is with Kevin Garnett (left) during a 2010 game. >>>

 A CELTIC STAR

The Celtics went from one of the worst NBA teams to the best team during Rondo's second year. In the 2007–2008 season, Rondo became the starting point guard. He was the leader of a team that included other great players such as Kevin Garnett, Ray Allen, and Paul Pierce.

The Celtics made it to the playoffs each year from 2008 until 2011. Here is Rondo (right) shooting against the Cleveland Cavaliers during the 2010 playoffs.

Rondo was still one of the youngest players on the team, but he led the Celtics through the **playoffs** and to the NBA Finals. The Finals are basketball's biggest **championship**. Rondo proved himself again in the Finals because the Celtics faced the Los Angeles Lakers, one of the NBA's strongest teams.

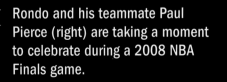

Rondo and his teammate Paul Pierce (right) are taking a moment to celebrate during a 2008 NBA Finals game.

17

ALL-STAR PLAYER

Playing the Lakers in the 2008 Finals put Rondo's leadership skills to the test. Many people thought the Lakers were the best team in the NBA. Rondo played some of his best basketball yet, and the Celtics won the Finals.

Since Boston is in the eastern part of the United States, Rondo has played for the Eastern Conference team in the All-Star Game. Here he is during the 2010 All-Star Game, which the Eastern Conference team won 141–139.

The Lakers' coach Phil Jackson said that the Celtics beat his team because of Rondo. Rondo was now one of the biggest stars in the NBA. He was voted an all-star in 2010 and played in his first All-Star Game. This is a special game in which only the biggest stars in basketball get to play. Most NBA players never get to play in an All-Star Game.

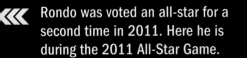

Rondo was voted an all-star for a second time in 2011. Here he is during the 2011 All-Star Game.

19

ASSISTING OFF THE COURT

Rondo helps his team score on the court. He helps others off the court. Rondo created the Assisting Youth Foundation to help children in poor areas. These children might live in bad neighborhoods with drugs and crime. They might go to failing schools. Rondo knows that they need help.

Rondo has also gone to events that supported other good causes. Here he is at a 2010 event that raised money for cancer research. >>>

The Assisting Youth Foundation is a **charity** that works in a very special way. People can give as little as $2 every time Rondo makes an assist for the Celtics. That money goes to help children in need. The money adds up fast because Rondo makes so many assists. The better he plays, the more children he helps!

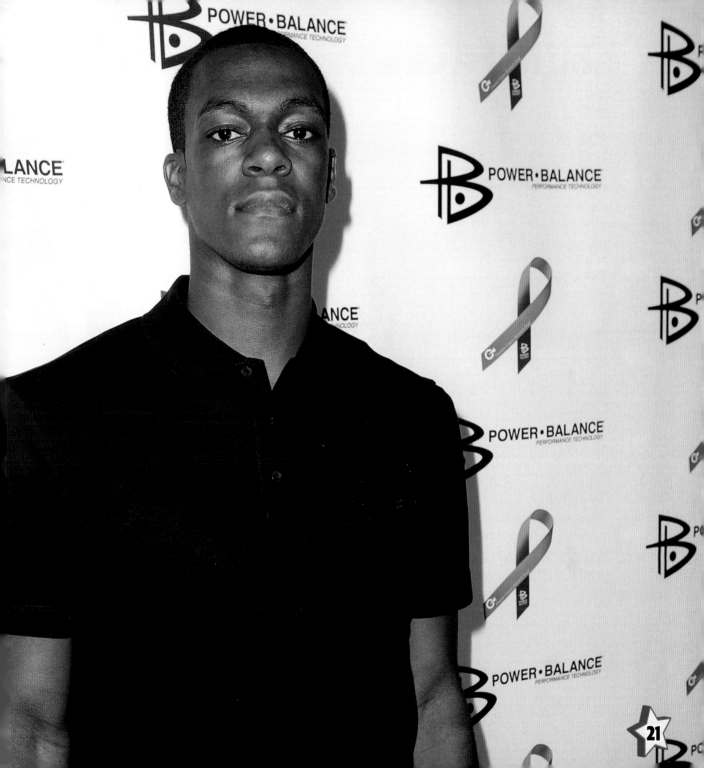

★ FUN FACTS

 Rondo's hands are so big that he earned the nickname E.T. E.T. is an alien from a movie. He has very big hands.

 One of Rondo's favorite foods is tacos.

 Rondo's favorite baseball team is the Boston Red Sox.

 Rondo might be famous, but he is also very shy.

 Rajon loved playing Connect Four with his family when he was growing up. He still plays it today.

 Rondo's favorite movie is *Love & Basketball*.

 Rondo holds Camp Rondo, at which he teaches children how to play basketball, every year.

 Rondo has more assists in the NBA Playoffs than any other Celtic in team history.

 Rondo set several records for the Kentucky Wildcats, including steals.

 Rondo is so good at making steals that basketball fans call him a thief.

GLOSSARY

championship (CHAM-pee-un-ship) A contest held to determine the best, or the winner.

charity (CHER-uh-tee) A group that gives help to the needy.

coach (KOHCH) A person who directs a team.

draft (DRAFT) The selection of people for a special purpose.

passing (PAS-ing) Handing the ball off to another player.

playoffs (PLAY-ofs) Games played after the regular season ends to see who will play in the championship game.

point guard (POYNT GAHRD) A basketball player who directs his or her team's forward plays on the court.

professional (pruh-FESH-nul) Someone who is paid for what he or she does.

rookies (RU-keez) New major-league players.

shoot (SHOOT) To throw a basketball toward the basket.

stealing (STEEL-ing) When a player takes the basketball from the other team.

INDEX

WEB SITES

Due to the changing nature of Internet links, PowerKids Press has developed an online list of Web sites related to the subject of this book. This site is updated regularly. Please use this link to access the list:
www.powerkidslinks.com/hero/rondo/